The Love of Dumdum

by Sandy Smith

The First Time

The first time that Dumdum came to our porch that Dumdum was Kelly's cat,

Kelly got Dumdum from a friend of Kelly's,

Kelly, named him Mr. Kitty,

When Chris and Kelly's second oldest brother was at our house Billy approached him inside our house,

None of us didn't want Dumdum to get hit or ran over,

So Dumdum became Chris and I's cat,

The first time Dumdum came in, Dumdum didn't know what to think,

Knowing that Chris fell in love with Dumdum instantly,

So Kelly let us keep Dumdum,

Chris decided to name the cat Dumdum because of the looks that Dumdum gave.

Even though Dumdum loved the outdoors. Even though Dumdum was

declawed that Dumdum got out.

Dumdum loved to explore the outside.

I Love You Mr. Kitty Dumdum Cline

Written On August 3rd, 2016

I thought we had you for 7 years,

We had you for 9 years,

We loved you from the start,

We didn't want you to go,

When you left us that we weren't ready to let you go,

We had our ups and downs,

Dumdum, I hope that you'll realize on how much I love you,

Like I told you,

You weren't supposed to go before us (your dad and I),

I want to tell you my dear sweet baby boy,

Where ever you are that I love you so much,

You didn't have to leave us so quickly,

Why did you have to leave us so quickly?,

Why did you have to go?,

Baby, I love you,

I know that I had mentioned that I am not ready to let you go,

My love for you will never fade away,

You have been the best cat that I could ever ask for,

You had made me laugh on the things you've done,

You tried to open doors and couldn't,

You loved your dad more than anything,

I know that you have a special bond for your dad and I,

Dumdum, I can't tell you on how much "I LOVE YOU",

I know that it's been the three of us,

The thing is though,

You kept us together all these years,

Dumdum, I want to say thank you for keeping your dad and I together,

You know how much that means to me,

I hope that you know how much that means to me,

Thank you baby,

We will always love you Dumdum.

Not A Day That Goes By

Not a day that goes by that your dad and I don't think about you,

We speak of you as much as we can possible,

Since your dad and I got Flash and Snoopy,

Flash tends to act like you Dumdum,

But with Flash that Flash doesn't give those looks like you did,

I'll never forget how you watched over Jessica Kirk oldest daughter,

You made sure the baby was fine,

Knowing that I'm drawing a blank on the oldest girls name,

You made sure no one didn't mess with your dad and your dad's oldest granddaughter.

There are days I think of you and your sister Sway,

On how much I miss you both,

Dumdum, you and Sway always had a way on how to make me smile,

I sure miss those days,

I wish that you and Sway were here,

I sure miss you Dumdum,

It's not the same without you Dumdum,

Knowing that you knew how to make your dad and I laugh,

The way you lay above your dad's head.

Dumdum please make sure to watch over your sister Sway,

Sway needs you the most,

Show Sway the guidance there in heaven,

Show Sway on how much you loved your dad and I,

Make sure to love your sister like you have for your dad and I,

Make sure to keep Sway safe,

Show Sway the tops on being safe,

Keep an eye on Sway,

Make sure to take care of Sway.

Rest In Peace Dumdum

I'll Never Forget

I'll never forget the time that I went to search for you,

I couldn't find you anywhere,

I had to wake your dad up,

Your dad and I looked everywhere for you,

Your dad found you on top of the refrigerator,

You Dumdum was such a snicker on hiding from your mom,

Even though I didn't put it the piece together until your dad told me on how you got up there on top of the refrigerator,

The freezer was nearby and you jumped onto the freezer and onto the refrigerator,

It made sense,

I couldn't help it but to take this picture of you Dumdum.

When that front door was opened that Dumdum loved looking out,

Dumdum always loved looking out and making sure no one came through that door,

Knowing that Chris and I always had the screen door locked,

Plus Dumdum loved the setup in the front room,

That way Dumdum can keep an eye on his (Dumdum's) parents.

Dumdum loved giving those looks.

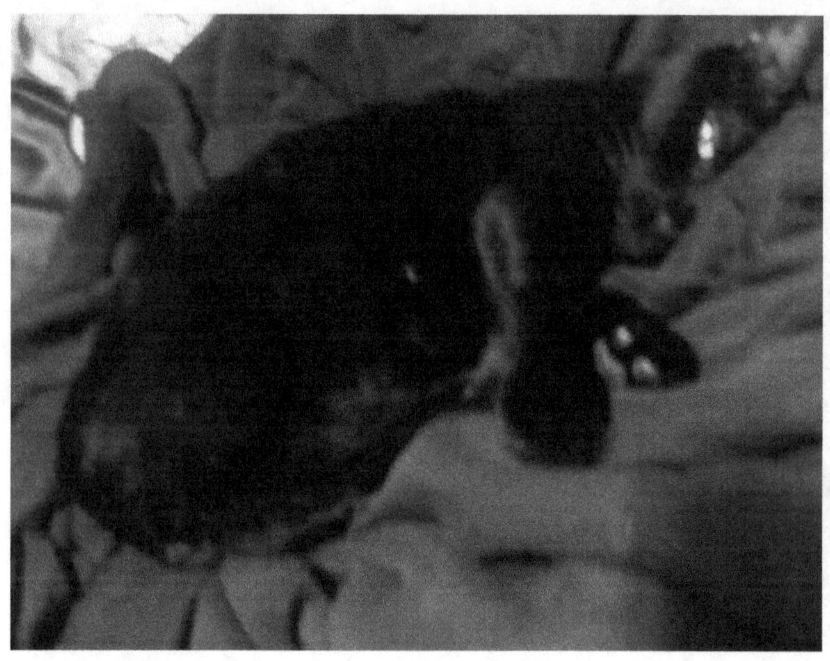

Dumdum loved being on the bed. Always loved being on daddy's side of the bed.

I'll Never Forget

Dumdum and Dumdum's mom was in the spare room,

There was a twin size bed that was in the spare room,

Dumdum's mom had stuffed animals on the bed that Dumdum's mom got over the years from Dumdum's dad,

Dumdum fall in love with the black doggy dog dog,

Knowing that Dumdum blend so well with the black doggy dog dog,

So Dumdum's mom decided to let Dumdum have the stuffed dog.

Tennis Ball

Dumdum's mom thought that Dumdum would love to play with the tennis ball,

The time that Dumdum's mom put the tennis ball down for Dumdum,

That Dumdum went crazy over the tennis ball.

Dumdum tends to give the look

Dumdum always loved being in the kitchen and watching Dumdum's mom cook as Dumdum's mom was in the kitchen.

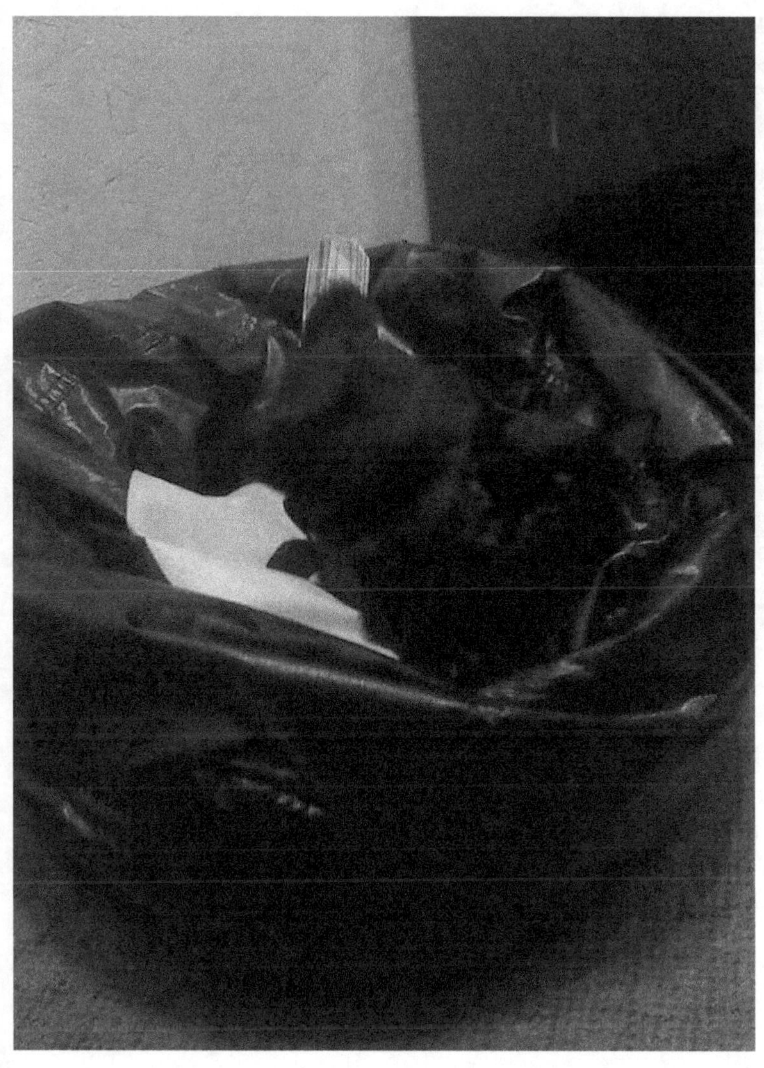

Dumdum always loved laying in Dumdum's dad's bean bag.

No matter what Dumdum loved being in any type boxes that comes into the house. Dumdum's parents remembered a time that Dumdum got into an empty 24 cardboard box of Coke Cola. It made Dumdum's parents laugh.

No matter what Dumdum loved his full attention from everyone

Dumdum loved being comfortable

Dumdum loved being at Dumdum's dad's legs, knee's and anywhere around Dumdum's dad. Dumdum was a daddy's boy.

Dumdum loved hiding

Dumdum “HATED” having Dumdum’s bath time. Dumdum always tries his best to escape from his mom.

In the spare bedroom that Dumdum was trying to catch a fly

Dumdum always loved being comfortable around Dumdum's dad

Wherever Dumdum's dad is that Dumdum is close to Dumdum's dad

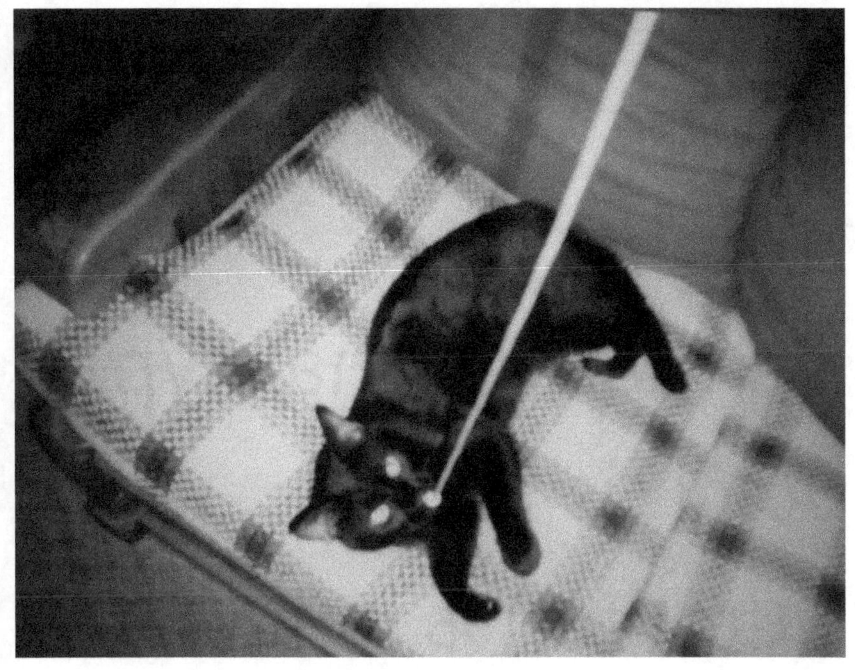

Dumdum loved playing with a string

No matter what type box it is that Dumdum is in it.

Coca-Cola

Coca-Cola

There was a time that Dumdum had his paws on the knob to get into the bedroom to be with Dumdum's dad. Dumdum almost had the knob turned to get into the bedroom. Dumdum was always a daddy's boy.

No matter what Dumdum always gave the orneriness looks

Dumdum didn't want mom to leave.

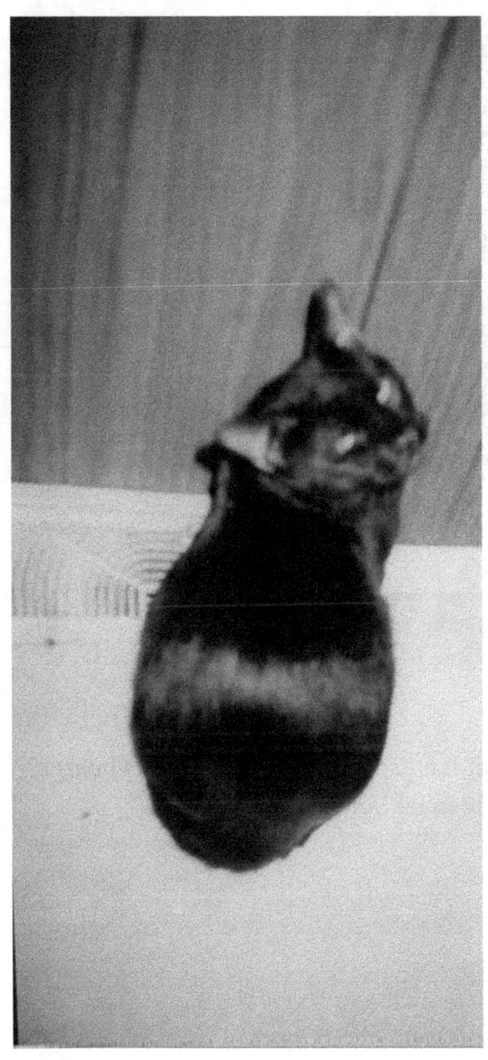

Dumdum always loved being close to the heat vent during the winter months

When Dumdum became sick that it crushed Dumdum's parents hearts. Dumdum's parents weren't ready to let Dumdum go.

No matter if it was Dumdum's daddy or mom that Dumdum gave these type of looks. Like are you crazy.

Dumdum always liked to get comfortable.

Dumdum tends to get these types of looks.

Dumdum loved the chair, Dumdum's dad's bean bag, Dumdum's mom's black stuffed animal, the rose's that you see, Dumdum's mom decided to put the biker bear that on the jacket that says I wuff you and the memory box that has Dumdum's pictures, Dumdum's tennis ball and other items in for Dumdum.

www.ingramcontent.com/pod-product-compliance
Lightning Source LLC
LaVergne TN
LVHW052106160826
845678LV00015B/3399